WISDOM WALK TALK

SOLACE

Copyright © 2024 by Sade Horsley/SOLACE.

All rights reserved. No part of this book may be reproduced in any form or by any electronic or mechanical means, including information storage and retrieval systems, without permission in writing from the publisher, except by reviewers, who may quote brief passages in a review.

This publication contains the opinions and ideas of its author. It is intended to provide helpful and informative material on the subjects addressed in the publication. The author and publisher specifically disclaim all responsibility for any liability, loss, or risk, personal or otherwise, which is incurred as a consequence, directly or indirectly, of the use and application of any of the contents of this book.

WRITERS REPUBLIC L.L.C.
515 Summit Ave. Unit R1
Union City, NJ 07087, USA

Website: *www.writersrepublic.com*
Hotline: *1-877-656-6838*
Email: *info@writersrepublic.com*

Ordering Information:
Quantity sales. Special discounts are available on quantity purchases by corporations, associations, and others. For details, contact the publisher at the address above.

Library of Congress Control Number:		2024949530
ISBN-13:	979-8-89100-736-9	[Paperback Edition]
	979-8-89100-737-6	[Hardback Edition]
	979-8-89100-738-3	[Digital Edition]

Rev. date: 11/19/2024

Greetings to all kinds and like minds, welcome to Solace Society, where whatever we may seek in life is meant to be.

All we ask is that you add your peace of perception as you take a walk with us amongst our wisdom walk.

Every little step we take we learn something, don't you agree? Being independent beings we can only use what we've experienced while sharing what we've learned along the way. No matter what path you choose to take in this realm, there will be obstacles to push through and get by. Speaking only from experience we can pry, cry or get by the key is to at least try! I've gladly decided to make the time to share my blueprint with you. The map to my wisdom walk, now enjoy this treasure with me while they still look for the gold in the Titanic.

I would like to give Gratitude to those who have helped me in putting this together as I am blessed to be surrounded by my spirit guides. This book is for everyone so don't be shy. Remember to always have your own voice. I am just here for you to hear you speak louder.

Shall we begin kin?

A

Accountability- Be fully accountable for all of your actions

Acknowledgement- Acknowledge the perspective of all beings and factors at all times

Action- Take the action to accept, don't expect and move on!

Analyze- Analyze the situation without ego and being persuaded by emotions.

Awareness- Heighten your awareness of your what's and why's…

B

Blink- Thr33 times to determine if it's worth a tear

Breathe- Remind yourself you're still here

Believe- Your Solar plexus (that gut feeling) will guide you!

Barter- What is in it for you? Is it worth your innergy? Referring to your " inner "G" for all the spiritual gangstas out there

Bondage- The Promise to SELF..consider this bondage for the better you.

A&B Solace Sought:

"Start your break thru it will regenerate the old you"

C

Commitment- In addition to the bondage to self, you must also know the importance of commitment to others when making a promise. "Word is bond..verbal bondage"

Comfortability- Try it. You never know what it can do for you.

Communication- Speak it, whatever it is that you feel and how you want or need it to be.

Consistency-Make it a routine, make it work!

Confidence- Make your choice with confidence and always be aware of the consequences.

C Solace Sought:

"Be comfortably committed to what you do while being confident and consistent in your communication"

Beyond the comfort zone:

"I am afraid of heights my subconscious said..until I was challenged by a friend of mine (Lucas) to bungee jump off a building at 855ft. Was I afraid, absolutely but once I jumped it was one of the most liberating feelings I have ever felt..No gravity. I was flying. Or as Woody would tell Buzz Lightyear, I was "falling — with style." It was similar to Batman; he doesn't fly — he soars!

"Be committed to your comfortability and communicate with confidence consistently" ✦

D

Destination: What is your destination of your wisdom walk? Are you unsure? No worries. It is destined to change according to what we grow through. Just stay focused and stay on your desired path.

Dominance: You are the only one that can control you — not others. If you have any children, this ultimately applies to them as well.

Develop: What are the end games for your goals, and do you have the blueprint for each one?

Discover: You will discover as you execute your plan!

Determine: Decide how you will go about getting there. Back to the basics (your blueprint!)

D Solace Sought:

Discover your destination and determine your development with dominance!

Let's pause for a moment. How is your spirit today? At your own pace, take three deep breaths

… Are you ready for what's next?

E

Examine- Every aspect of the outcome

Entertain- Which perception makes the most sense to you? (positive thoughts only)

Exhale- Breathe it out and inner stand your decision

Elevate- Ascend from your choice of lesson

Educate yourself and others by sharing your working results amongst your wisdom walk.

E Solace Sought:

Expectations can lead to humble destruction. Just know the results may not be what you want in the moment but it shall benefit you in the long run!

Cool down eye feel you igniting! Think for a second..

"Be aware of those who pause your wisdom walk, ask yourself are they worth the next block"

Who do you feel owes you a thank you, and why?

List three people and reasons here:

F

Fight your initial reaction internally before it's expressed externally (take three breaths)

Flipping the fuck out is necessary sometimes.. yes I said it! (Tantrums may occur but a yell or scream is permitted whenever you need it)

Find the foundation of fuck it/forget it and let it go

Fin- Finish/Finito, once it's done come to closure it's imperative that you do.

Free your mind, body and soul from long term baggage/aged bags from carrying old shit!

Cool down you're lighting up..

What are three things that you fear?

G

Growth: How much has your mindset grown over time? How aware are you of the growth you need to make going forward?

Gratitude: Always thank those that have blessed you amongst your wisdom walk.

Gratefulness: Be grateful you have the ability to learn and comprehend whatever is at hand.

Grasp: Hone the ability to comprehend the lessons learned throughout your wisdom walk and the gifts that you obtain.

Gain: Acquire the strength to remain as strong as you are right now and going forward. (My mom has been diagnosed with Multiple Sclerosis for some time now, and if she can do it, so can you) Indefinitely!

G Solace Sought:

Grudges are feelings you continue to hold on to from others' past mistakes. Let those go! Don't YOU make a mistake by holding onto their MISSED TAKES!!

H

Hazards- Come in all disguises, open your eyes and recognize them.

Home- Maintain your sanctuary, living space to declutter and maintain a clear mindset at all times

Habitat- Connect with nature and your primal instincts, what lies inside you.

Health- Know your body what harms or helps in all aspects (your body is truly your temple)

Humble- Remain humble to 🐻 bear witness to your own growth and reflect upon it.

Next I want to share one of my mantras that helped me face my truths in the most productive way:

Are you honest with yourself?"

To enemies you are upfront, To friends you are loyal, To companions you are true, Are you honest with yourself?

"As physical beings we are here to make mistakes. If we have morals and keep mistakes to a minimum we will be able to manifest the environment and desires we need."

What do you consider your strongest desire? Why do you think that is, is it attainable? If not, perhaps you might want to reconsider your strongest desire. if so, how do you plan to attain it?

I

Idea: Ideas come from within. Being your own creative self is not a sin.

Intelligence: Research, confirm your resources, and record your experience (what you have learned).

Information: All information regarding your "soul-called" ideas is only for you unless you choose to share, but be aware of whom you share with.

Imperative: It is imperative to know all that involves you. Be aware at all times.

Install: Install your self love drive like a USB -- in and out gracefully without causing damage to self and others. What would be the use of a damaged hard drive?

Take care of yourself like you do your phone. You always have the right case and battery charger right? You need to apply that to everyday life!

I Solace Sought:

The infinity symbol ∞: the number "8" shape never stops or takes a break -- it is ongoing and it keeps flowing.

J

Justify- Is it in your favor, remove your ego. What do you truly think?

Judgement- Scales..what matters to you most, is it logical?

Jealousy- Why? What is in you that caused this reaction? Time to reevaluate…Jealousy is a natural reaction yet you must expel it immediately!

Jargon- What is your choice of dialect and tone to deal with difficult situations?

Learn that and choose that every time to keep it consistent.

Joke- It is healthy to laugh yet be mindful when making jokes and be aware if you lie to yourself or others.

K

Knowledge: What you learn ... apply it when you are certain it is known and true!

King: Adopt your king innergy (inner G") to be able to lead, listen and follow.

Kindle: Kindle sparked flames within you, and with control. Don't let anyone put out your flame.

Kindness: Even if not reciprocated, being kind brings continual blessings your way. Start counting now!

Know: Know what you are doing, what you have done, and what is next for you (refer to your blueprint). Know that whatever it may be, it is meant for you, and you set the life laws for self. Know your control and your limitations. KNOW YOU! Know this and notice the new you. Learn the new you.

L

Learn- The value of you

Listen- To what the most high and spirit guides are communicating to you

Language- is displayed in a variety of ways: body, speech and actions. Are you multilingual?

Love- The spirit within and the human connection you are connected with.

Levitate and elevate with the new foundation of awareness, continue to create opportunities for the unseen.

M

Mistake- "Miss Take" it again until you win

Minimum- Plan minimum and execute to the maximum

Morals- Respect, reciprocation of service, love, positive innergy are necessities in life to keep the vibes right.

Magick- Do you believe in the magic that you obtain? Tap in and you'll find that we are all mystical, trust me!

Manage- Manage all that requires order: time, money, family, work, life..one day at a time.

Lists are a great way to keep on top of your tasks.

What are five of your morals?

N

Nature- Will give you the answers that you long for..Close your mouth and open your ears. She is talking to you, do you hear it?

Nurture- All of you inside and out that's what true self love is all about!

Notice (Know this)- All the potential you possess makes you limitless!

Navigate-Pay attention to all surroundings and settings at all times.

Nothing- It is ok to do nothing, silence yourself and your thoughts. Being silent can assist in active listening as we all need to do just a little bit more.

How much time do you spend in nature?

What type of nature brings you the most serenity?

O

Ostracize- Your spirit and mindset whenever you feel necessary

Organize- Your own healthy choices for self and connections

Obtain- The required assets

Observe- What ostracizing and organizing helps improve

Own Your Shit- Be Responsible and able to communicate your faults if any in all situations.

O Solace Sought:

"Overstand how far you have gone and inner stand where you are about to go."

P

Personal- How much does it truly have to do with you personally? Ask yourself, am I projecting my emotions into this situation?

Preference- Gives you power and independence in your choice. Would you rather quit or deal with it?

Perception- Is it clear, is your perception causing reactions solely from your trauma triggers?

Pride- Put your pride aside and then decide..

Protection- Protect all of you when making your final decision!

Use whatever spiritual guidance or self recollection you feel you need for protection in all aspects.

P Solace sought:

"It's your personal preference of your perception to maintain pride and create your own form of protection"
-Solace

Q

Quiet: Quiet can seem unbearable at times, but this is when you connect with your subconscious — uninterrupted.

Quirky: Being who you are is absolutely fine. Always embrace your authenticity! Did you remind yourself that you love you today?

Question: Question your space (relationship status) with others — especially family when you feel necessary. A simple, "how are you?" or, "are we okay?" can go along way.

Queen: Embody the queen in thou, and be proud of that Crown! (Fellas, we all have a little of both in us — it's the innergy that you are attracted to. not at all trying to offend you. Truce?)

Qi: Maintain balance with your innergy. Keep your positive innergy in tact. Be strong enough to have your own back.

R

Replenish: Refill your innergy and purify as needed. Clear storage within the cranium and cache as you do your electronic devices.

Resilience: Resilience is a tool that is so powerful and underrated. Practice resilience to avoid a toxic relationship, reaction and/or situation.

Realize: Realize the growth that just took place while reading and applying this handbook. Applaud yourself for getting this far! Thank you, by the way, I am grateful!

Review: Review the process of your growth. Keep track of where you have flourished and conquered.

Rewind: Take a second and look back. Where were you on this day last year? How much progress have you or haven't you made?

S

Stability: What we chase with focus we can always maintain.

Strength: Strength Is not always meant to be physical. Psychologically, we are stronger than a golden glove champ. Keep that in mind and keep training self to be better than yesterday.

Satisfy: "Satisfy Your Soul" — inspired by Bob Marley — with the outcome and continue toward it until you achieve what is right for you.

Solidify: Solidify the challenge. Break it down into sections, and take it one step at a time.

Moderation is great to practice and experience, let me tell you!

Stop: Stop self from blaming others. Question self primarily. "Is there a lesson in this for me?"

What is your Solace (comfort in a time of distress)?

T

Truth: Truth to self — most of us run from. It's okay, I'll say it for you. More importantly, truth outside of yourself is truly valuable.

As Pharrell said, "The truth will piss you off then set you free". Do you agree?

Trial: Trial as if every action is being judged by your subconscious jury. You are your own judge and use your scales wisely.

Train: Train your ego to work with you — not against you … it could be your biggest blessing blocker.

Teach: Teach others what you have learned along the way to maintain the cycle of worldly healing.

Treatment: Use all that positively works for you. What is your formula?

U

Utilize: Utilize your knowledge to connect with your Higher Being and receive the answers you need.

Unrealistic: Be content with the outcome even if it's not how you desired it to be. (See E in booklet)

Understand: Understand self, your wisdom walk, and your growth. Know eye before any.

Unlearn: Unlearn how you were yesterday to give birth to the new you today!

Universe: The Universe Is always walking, watering, and working with you. Stay alert!

"Be grateful and thankful for the Universe, as it's U.N.I. VS THE WORLD"

V

Vitalize- Body, show self care that you are still progressing and still here for another year! Happy birthday, even if it's not continue to celebrate you!

Vision- Use your vision as a sense of premonition. Your eyes are the mirror to your soul. Go within and watch the greatness unfold.

"If you wanna be somebody if you wanna go somewhere ... you better wake up and pay attention"
-Sister Act 2 (1993)

What I am saying is,

Use your eyes to see what is best for you. If you pay attention, your vision will show you the way.

Versatile- Be different with your approach and be unforgettably incomparable, be noticed!

Vapors- Sometimes you have to ghost (disappear on people or toxic situations). Trust it's permitted, we are all adults here. You can explain later–yet it's all up to you.

Visualize-If it is worth your time, innergy and effort. Where do you see this going in reality not your own fantasy world.

W

Wander: Find a new environment, spaces, and places to unleash the true you!

Wait: Wait for the results you want. It will take patience, but you got this!

Watch: Watch the Universe as it reacts to your magic, dedication, and effort.

Want: Want more for your well being. Do not settle if it's not enough for you!

Withhold: Withhold some experiences for self at times. The celebration is you! As the old saying goes, "Don't put all your eggs in one basket."

Solace says, "I'm still learning…"

X

Xyster: It's required to stay at ease while going thru your transformation. Smooth it out. Just take it all with grace and moderation.

Xylose: Do not ever dilute or hollow out the best of you for anyone or anything other than self.

Xylem: Maintain the body with proper spiritual nutrients from head to toe. Practice your chakras, pray more — whatever it may be — and keep it spiritually healthy.

Y

You: YOU come first at all times — take it or leave it!

Youth: Stay as young as you can for as long as you can. "I don't wanna grow up. I'm a TOYS R US kid."

They told us. We didn't listen. Boy I wish I did. Innocence is purity in alignment with playful innergy. Trouble comes with a conscience.

Z

Zenith: Reach for the peak of your greatness. You deserve it! Truth, love, and magic is within you. EMBRACE IT!

Wowwww…yayy you took this wisdom walk with me. I could not be more GRATEFUL! We are forever reconnected and I want to share this perspective with you:

What if we were to go back to the basics … childhood, to be specific. Would you consider your legos to be the foundation of life? Can you see the comparison?

Brainstorm on this question a bit. Feel free to use the journal space provided for a response.

How do you utilize your Legos in life:

Do you Lego and build a new foundation?

OR

Do you "Leg-go" & Let's go — time to move forward and ascend?

Which ones speaks the most to you? Apply that, thank me later.

Love yourself more than anything else. If you are looking for love, look in here, or look in the mirror it's right there!!!

Eye am more than grateful and proud of you for finishing this project! Proud of me for having the discipline to complete it as procrastination is the ex with the best. WATCH YOUR MOUTH! Truly my goal is to reach one soul whether it'd be you or who you passed this book to. As this is a token of gratitude from me to you, I would love for you to do the same thing too.

Lastly,

A.R.E (Ascension, Reflect, Expect)

Ascension is necessary as you rise above and get over any obstacle in life. Let's elevate and levitate!

Reflect on what's next

What do you Expect from you?

Sending Solace vibes your way in all ways, always ;)

Again, welcome to Solace Soci3ty. Throughout the completion of this project, I released my mother to another realm. However, I have gained my favorite angel along with other loved ones. I say this to myself daily:

"I did not lose my mother, I let her go.

Eye am not lost without her, as I have gained guidance.

Now eye have no option of cant.

Eye have to raise myself.

-SolAce #SolaceSoci3ty #wisdomwalktalk

Wisdom Walk Reflection Section

Milton Keynes UK
Ingram Content Group UK Ltd.
UKHW041151051224
451950UK00038B/142/J